The 111 Regrets Reflection Workbook

The 111 Regrets Reflection Workbook

Guided Questions to Help You Reflect, Learn, and Live Without Regrets

Aria Capri Publishing Group
Mauricio Vasquez

Toronto, Canada

The 111 Regrets Reflection Workbook by Aria Capri Publishing Group (Aria Capri International Inc.). All Rights Reserved.

You may reproduce no other parts of this publication in whole or in part, shared with others, stored in a retrieval system, digitized, or transmitted in any form without written permission from the publisher.

Copyright © 2025, Aria Capri Publishing Group (Aria Capri International Inc.). All rights reserved.

Authors:
Aria Capri Publishing Group
Mauricio Vasquez

First Printing: March 2025

978-1-998729-17-3 (Hardcover book)
978-1-998729-16-6 (Paperback)

Deepen Your Reflection & Take Action

Thank you for choosing The 111 Regrets Reflection Workbook! This workbook is designed to help you reflect on life's most common regrets and make meaningful changes. But reflection is just the first step—understanding the psychological foundations behind these regrets and learning actionable strategies can empower you to transform your life.

To help you on this journey, I've created the book '111 Most Common Regrets of the Dying That You Can Avoid Today':

✔ Explore the psychology behind each regret – Understand why these regrets are so common and how they shape our lives.

✔ Discover the consequences of inaction – Learn what happens when these regrets are left unaddressed.

✔ Get 3 powerful strategies for each regret – Practical steps to help you avoid or overcome these regrets before it's too late.

Your journey to a life of purpose, fulfillment, and fewer regrets starts here.

Scan now to unlock deeper insights and strategies for intentional living!

Share Your Experience & Help Others

If this workbook has helped you reflect and grow, your review can inspire others to start their own journey.

Scan the QR code to leave a review – It takes just a minute, but your words can make a big impact!

Thank you for your support!

Introduction: How to Use This Workbook

Regret is a universal human experience. It reflects our deepest values, missed opportunities, and unspoken words. But regret doesn't have to be a burden—it can be a powerful teacher. This workbook is designed to help you reflect, learn, and take action so that you can make choices today that lead to a life with fewer regrets.

This workbook is a companion guide to explore 111 of the most common regrets people have at the end of their lives. Each page is dedicated to one specific regret, accompanied by three carefully crafted reflection questions. These questions are designed to prompt deep self-reflection, spark personal insights, and inspire meaningful change.

How to Use This Workbook

1. Set Your Own Pace
   - You don't have to complete this book in one sitting. Take your time, focusing on one regret at a time or flipping through and choosing those that resonate with you the most.
2. Engage in Honest Reflection
   - Each regret includes three reflection questions. Use them as prompts for journaling, deep thinking, or even discussing with a trusted friend or mentor.
   - Be honest with yourself—this is a judgment-free space for self-awareness and growth.
3. Write, Express, and Plan
   - Use the space provided to write your thoughts, emotions, and action steps.
   - You might notice patterns in your responses—areas where you wish to change, improve, or take action.
4. Take Small but Meaningful Action
   - Awareness is powerful, but action creates transformation. As you go through the workbook, identify one small action you can take today to avoid experiencing that regret later in life.
5. Revisit and Reflect
   - Over time, your answers may evolve. Use this workbook as a living document, revisiting previous regrets and reflections to see how your perspective changes.

Your Journey Toward a Life Without Regrets

This workbook is not about dwelling on the past—it's about shaping the future. The insights you gain here are an opportunity to make better decisions, strengthen relationships, and live with intention. By working through these pages, you are taking a powerful step toward a life of fulfillment, clarity, and peace.

Now, let's begin.

Disclaimer

The content of this book is intended for informational and reflective purposes only. It does not constitute legal, financial, medical, or psychological advice and should not be relied upon as a substitute for professional guidance. The insights and reflections contained within are based on common themes of human experience and should not be interpreted as specific recommendations for any individual situation.

Neither the author nor the publisher makes any representations or warranties regarding the accuracy, applicability, or completeness of the information provided. Any decisions, actions, or inactions taken based on the content of this book are the sole responsibility of the reader. The author and publisher disclaim all liability for any direct, indirect, incidental, consequential, or special damages arising from the use, misuse, or inability to use this material, including but not limited to emotional distress, financial losses, health-related decisions, personal relationships, or any other outcomes resulting from actions taken or not taken based on the content of this book. The reader assumes full responsibility for any choices made as a result of engaging with this material.

If you are experiencing distress, mental health concerns, or any medical condition, it is strongly advised that you seek the assistance of a qualified healthcare provider, therapist, or other relevant professional. This book is not intended to diagnose, treat, cure, or prevent any condition and should not replace professional medical or psychological support.

Furthermore, the author and publisher do not assume responsibility for how this book is used, interpreted, or applied by any reader. Any reliance on the information herein is at the reader's own risk. If you are in crisis or require immediate assistance, please seek professional help or contact emergency services.

Your well-being is important. Please use this book as a tool for reflection and self-awareness, but always prioritize professional advice when needed.

1. NOT SPENDING ENOUGH TIME WITH LOVED ONES (FAMILY AND FRIENDS)

1. When I reflect on my calendar for the past month, what percentage of my discretionary time was deliberately allocated to deepening relationships with those I most value?
2. Which relationships in my life are at risk of weakening due to insufficient investment, and what specific "protected time" could I establish this week to begin strengthening these connections?
3. If my future self were to look back on my current relationship patterns, what adjustments would they most wish I had made today to create a foundation for lasting connection?

2. TAKING LOVED ONES FOR GRANTED AND FAILING TO APPRECIATE THEM

1. When was the last time I expressed specific, detailed appreciation to each of the most important people in my life, and what qualities or actions might I have overlooked?
2. What daily or weekly ritual could I establish to interrupt hedonic adaptation and maintain conscious awareness of the value others bring to my life?
3. Which relationships am I most likely taking for granted right now, and what novel expression of gratitude might reconnect me with their significance?

3. NOT EXPRESSING LOVE AND AFFECTION OPENLY TO THOSE WHO MATTERED

1. What specific fears or hesitations prevent me from expressing authentic affection more freely, and how might I begin addressing these barriers?
2. Who in my life might be uncertain about how deeply I care for them, and what mode of expression (verbal, written, physical) would most effectively communicate my feelings?
3. How might I gradually expand my emotional vocabulary and comfort with vulnerability to create more meaningful connections with those I value?

4. NOT SAYING "I LOVE YOU" ENOUGH TO MY FAMILY AND FRIENDS

1. When I consider those closest to me, with whom have I been most reluctant to verbalize love, and what meaning might my explicit expression hold for them?
2. What daily transition points (morning greeting, ending phone calls, bedtime) could serve as natural anchors for incorporating "I love you" more consistently?
3. How might the explicit verbalization of love—even when I believe it's understood—create security and connection that non-verbal expressions alone cannot provide?

5. NOT APOLOGIZING OR MAKING AMENDS WHEN I HURT SOMEONE DEAR

1. What unresolved conflicts or offenses am I currently carrying, and how might these appear insignificant from a future perspective while still causing present relationship damage?
2. In conflicts where I've contributed to harm, what prevents me from initiating reconciliation, and how does this reluctance align with my values about relationships?
3. How might I create a structured approach to apology that includes acknowledging specific harm, expressing genuine remorse, offering appropriate reparation, and committing to changed behavior?

6. HOLDING ONTO GRUDGES AND NOT FORGIVING LOVED ONES

1. What resentments am I currently maintaining, and what neurological and physiological costs might this continuous maintenance be extracting from my wellbeing?
2. How might understanding the contextual factors influencing others' hurtful behaviors help me develop a more nuanced perspective that facilitates forgiveness?
3. What would shift if I redefined forgiveness as an act of emotional liberation for myself rather than a statement about the offender's worthiness?

7. NOT FORGIVING MYSELF FOR MISTAKES THAT HURT MY RELATIONSHIPS

1. Where am I currently applying harsher standards to my own relationship mistakes than I would to someone else making similar errors?
2. How might recognizing the universality of human error—that imperfection is an inevitable aspect of being human—create psychological space for self-compassion?
3. What specific commitments to different future actions could help me move from unproductive self-punishment toward constructive growth?

8. LOSING TOUCH WITH CLOSE FRIENDS OVER THE YEARS

1. Which meaningful friendships have gradually faded from my life due to passive neglect rather than deliberate choice?
2. What specific, sustainable maintenance strategies (monthly calls, annual gatherings, regular check-ins) could I implement to preserve connections despite life transitions?
3. As I consider my current friendship patterns, how am I balancing immediate responsibilities against the long-term investment that lasting friendships require?

9. NOT BEING FULLY PRESENT WHEN SPENDING TIME WITH FAMILY

1. During recent family interactions, what percentage of my attention was genuinely focused on connection versus diverted by distractions, devices, or mental preoccupation?
2. What specific environmental adjustments (device-free zones, pre-interaction mental resets) would enhance my capacity for full presence during family time?
3. How might deliberately practicing uni-tasking—doing just one thing with complete attention—strengthen my ability to be fully present in my most important relationships?

10. PUTTING WORK OR OTHER OBLIGATIONS BEFORE FAMILY TIME

1. What implicit messages about priority and value am I communicating through my pattern of choosing work over family engagements?
2. Where in my schedule could I create better integration between work and family rather than treating them as competing priorities?
3. What brief transition ritual could help me shift psychological presence when moving between professional and family contexts?

11. NOT BEING A BETTER SPOUSE OR PARTNER (LACK OF EFFORT, UNDERSTANDING, OR COMMITMENT)

1. What regular investments am I making in relationship maintenance during non-crisis periods, and how do these align with research on relationship flourishing?
2. How attentively do I respond to my partner's "bids for connection" (attempts to engage, share, or connect), and what patterns might I notice about when I turn toward versus away from these opportunities?
3. In what ways could I more effectively serve as an emotional buffer, actively helping my partner navigate stressors through consistent support?

12. NOT BEING A BETTER PARENT (MISSING IMPORTANT MOMENTS IN MY CHILDREN'S LIVES)

1. What developmental windows or milestone opportunities with my children might I be undervaluing in my current time allocation decisions?
2. How effectively am I validating my children's emotions rather than dismissing them, and what impact might this have on their sense that their experiences matter?
3. What predictable routines or rituals could I establish around transitions (bedtime, meals, milestones) to provide security while creating memory anchors that strengthen family identity?

13. NOT BEING A BETTER SON OR DAUGHTER (NEGLECTING MY PARENTS WHEN THEY NEEDED ME)

1. How actively am I soliciting and preserving my parents' stories and experiences, recognizing that this family history would otherwise be lost?
2. What regular communication rhythms (weekly calls, monthly visits) could increase relationship satisfaction compared to sporadic, crisis-driven contact?
3. How collaboratively am I approaching care planning discussions, involving my parents in decisions about their needs and preferences rather than making unilateral choices?

14. ALLOWING PRIDE OR FEAR TO PREVENT ME FROM SAVING AN IMPORTANT RELATIONSHIP

1. What relationships in my life remain in "emotional gridlock"—a state of unresolved tension—because pride prevents me from initiating repair?
2. How would adopting a distant future perspective ("How will this matter in five years?") shift my willingness to prioritize relationship restoration over short-term ego protection?
3. What graduated contact approach (beginning with written communication before attempting in-person reconciliation) might reduce anxiety while increasing repair success?

15. LETTING A TRUE LOVE SLIP AWAY AND NOT FIGHTING FOR THAT RELATIONSHIP

1. What role has fear of vulnerability played in my reluctance to fully invest in promising relationships, and how has this affected my relationship satisfaction?
2. How might reframing relationship commitment as a choice made despite normal uncertainty, rather than waiting for perfect certainty, change my approach to romantic connection?
3. If I imagined my future self reflecting on my current relationship decisions, what advice might they offer about balancing protective caution against the risk of missed connection?

16. NOT HAVING THE COURAGE TO OPEN MY HEART FULLY TO LOVE (FEAR OF VULNERABILITY)

1. What early experiences may have taught me that emotional openness leads to rejection or invalidation, and how relevant are these lessons to my current relationships?
2. How might graduated emotional disclosure—sharing increasingly personal information in manageable steps—help build my vulnerability tolerance while minimizing anxiety?
3. What trusted relationships could serve as "secure bases" where I might practice greater emotional openness, gradually expanding my capacity for vulnerability?

17. NOT REACHING OUT TO RECONCILE WITH ESTRANGED FAMILY MEMBERS OR FRIENDS SOONER

1. What assumptions about rejection or futility might be preventing me from attempting reconciliation with estranged loved ones?
2. How might approaching reconciliation as a process rather than an event, with modest initial goals focused on communication rather than immediate closeness, increase the likelihood of successful reconnection?
3. What thoughtfully composed written initiation might allow for careful consideration of tone while giving the recipient space to process before responding?

18. CAUSING PAIN TO LOVED ONES THROUGH MY ACTIONS AND NOT MAKING IT RIGHT

1. Where have I caused harm in relationships without taking full responsibility, and what keeps me from addressing these situations?
2. How completely do my apologies typically include all five components of effective repair: acknowledging specific harm, expressing genuine remorse, explaining without excuse, offering reparation, and committing to behavior change?
3. How might distinguishing shame ("I am bad") from guilt ("I did something bad") increase my willingness to address relationship harm?

19. NOT SUPPORTING OR ENCOURAGING MY LOVED ONES' DREAMS AND GOALS

1. How often do I respond to others' aspirations with doubt rather than support, and what assumptions about risk or success underlie these responses?
2. In what ways could focusing encouragement on effort and strategy rather than innate talent better support persistence and resilience in my loved ones' goal pursuit?
3. How might curious questioning about possibilities, rather than immediate problem-identification, create psychological safety for dream-sharing?

20. FAILING TO CREATE SPECIAL MEMORIES OR TRADITIONS WITH MY FAMILY

1. What consistent, repeating experiences have I established that build family identity and cohesion, and where might there be opportunities for meaningful additions?
2. How am I balancing material resource allocation versus experience investments, recognizing research showing the latter yields greater and more lasting happiness returns?
3. What documentation methods (photographs, journals, storytelling) might enhance the psychological impact of family experiences by creating opportunities for reminiscence?

21. STAYING TOO LONG IN AN UNHEALTHY OR TOXIC RELATIONSHIP INSTEAD OF LEAVING SOONER

1. Where in my relationships do I see evidence of "sunk cost fallacy"—continuing investment despite evidence of harm due to resources already expended?
2. How explicitly have I evaluated my relationships against my personal values rather than emotions or history?
3. What connections outside potentially problematic relationships could provide both practical assistance and perspective if transitions become necessary?

22. WORKING TOO MUCH AND MISSING OUT ON LIFE'S IMPORTANT MOMENTS

1. How accurately does my current time allocation reflect what I claim are my priorities, and where do the most significant discrepancies appear?
2. What would change if I conceptualized time as abundant rather than scarce, potentially enhancing both generosity with time and subsequent satisfaction?
3. How fully do I engage during non-work time—without digital distractions or mental preoccupation with work—to create relationship benefits disproportionate to time invested?

23. PUTTING CAREER AND SUCCESS AHEAD OF FAMILY AND PERSONAL LIFE

1. In what ways am I overestimating the impact of professional success on my overall happiness while underestimating adaptation effects?
2. How deliberately am I cultivating all five well-being dimensions (Positive emotion, Engagement, Relationships, Meaning, Achievement) rather than focusing predominantly on achievement?
3. What non-negotiable time blocks for family and personal renewal could I establish to protect these domains from professional encroachment?

24. STAYING IN A JOB I DISLIKED OUT OF COMFORT OR FEAR OF CHANGE

1. How accurately am I predicting potential regret from action (making a change) versus inaction (maintaining the status quo), and might I be overestimating one while underestimating the other?
2. How would writing about my life from a future perspective clarify which present choices I'm likely to regret?
3. What smaller career changes might I make before contemplating major transitions, providing valuable information about preferences and capacities while building confidence?

25. NOT PURSUING THE CAREER PATH OR DREAM JOB I TRULY WANTED

1. To what extent have external factors (salary, prestige, others' expectations) influenced my career decisions compared to intrinsic motivation?
2. How aligned is my current work with my signature strengths, and what opportunities might exist to apply these strengths more consistently?
3. What specific career identities have I been curious about but avoided exploring, and what limited experimentation might provide crucial data for more authentic choices?

26. NOT TAKING RISKS OR MAKING BOLD MOVES IN MY CAREER WHEN I HAD THE CHANCE

1. Which potential career opportunities have I avoided due to fear of uncertainty, and how might these appear from a future perspective?
2. What decision framework focused on minimizing future regret ("Which choice might I most regret not taking?") would help evaluate current opportunities?
3. How might deliberately exposing myself to small failures while practicing constructive responses enhance my capacity for calculated risks?

27. CHASING MONEY AND STATUS INSTEAD OF MEANINGFUL, FULFILLING WORK

1. To what extent do external rewards (salary, status) currently drive my career decisions versus intrinsic satisfaction?
2. How might reshaping my current role to incorporate more strengths use, purpose orientation, and positive relationships enhance meaning regardless of occupation?
3. What internal markers of fulfillment (engagement, accomplishment, learning) could I attend to more deliberately rather than focusing primarily on external validation?

28. NOT STARTING THE BUSINESS OR PASSION PROJECT I ALWAYS DREAMED OF

1. What smallest possible step toward my entrepreneurial vision could I execute immediately to reduce procrastination while providing critical feedback?
2. How might reframing setbacks as inevitable components of the entrepreneurial process rather than personal inadequacy increase my persistence?
3. What small, consistent actions could gradually incorporate my entrepreneurial identity into my self-concept, increasing the likelihood of sustained effort?

29. REMAINING TOO LONG IN A TOXIC OR STRESSFUL WORK ENVIRONMENT

1. What comprehensive costs (health impacts, relationship strain, emotional depletion) am I incurring by remaining in my current environment, and how do these compare to the perceived benefits?
2. What mindfulness techniques might help create emotional distance while facilitating clearer decision-making about potential transitions?
3. What resources outside my work environment (professional connections, financial reserves, emotional support) could I cultivate to increase my capacity for necessary changes?

30. NOT SETTING BOUNDARIES, ALLOWING WORK TO CONSUME MY LIFE

1. What specific technology-free times and spaces could I establish to reduce work intrusions while enhancing recovery experiences?
2. What deliberate psychological shifts between work and personal roles (changing clothes, brief meditation, physical activity) might enhance my presence in both domains?
3. How might defining boundaries based on explicit values rather than external expectations increase both my boundary maintenance and satisfaction with work-life integration?

31. TAKING TOO FEW BREAKS OR VACATIONS, ALWAYS BEING "ON THE JOB"

1. How might strategic breaks throughout my workday (5-15 minutes every 90 minutes) enhance both productivity and creativity compared to continuous effort?
2. What would make my vacation time truly restorative, involving complete disconnection from work to provide crucial cognitive and emotional reset?
3. What brief pleasurable activities could I incorporate throughout daily routines to create cumulative restorative benefits?

32. BURNING OUT BY PUSHING MYSELF TOO HARD AT WORK

1. How effectively am I attending to physical fundamentals (sleep, nutrition, exercise) and emotional wellbeing to create sustainable performance?
2. In what areas might strategic underachievement—deliberately selecting domains for excellence versus adequacy—reduce burnout risk while enhancing overall effectiveness?
3. How strongly is my work connected to personally significant values and impact that provide motivational sustainability beyond achievement-based drives?

33. NOT ALIGNING MY WORK WITH MY VALUES AND PASSIONS

1. What core values matter most deeply to me, and how well does my current work express or violate these values?
2. What elements of my current role could I reshape to incorporate more personal values and strengths without changing positions?
3. How might I actively connect my existing work to personally meaningful outcomes beyond immediate tasks to enhance purpose?

34. CHOOSING MY CAREER BASED ON OTHERS' EXPECTATIONS, NOT MY OWN DESIRES

1. To what extent was my career path chosen after sufficient exploration of personal interests and values versus responding to external expectations?
2. How effectively have I separated self-worth from external validation in making career decisions?
3. What personally meaningful elements could I gradually introduce into my current work before contemplating major transitions?

35. NOT USING MY TALENTS AND POTENTIAL TO THE FULLEST IN MY WORK

1. Which signature strengths am I underutilizing in my current role, and what opportunities might exist to apply them more consistently?
2. How often do I view abilities as developable through effort rather than fixed traits, and how does this perspective affect my willingness to embrace challenges?
3. What projects slightly beyond my current abilities could I select to create optimal conditions for both skill development and increased confidence?

36. LETTING FEAR OF FAILURE KEEP ME STUCK IN A SAFE CAREER

1. What specific fears are keeping me in my current position, and how realistic are these concerns when systematically evaluated?
2. How might reconceptualizing setbacks as learning opportunities rather than character indictments affect my willingness to pursue growth-oriented risks?
3. How would separating my identity from outcomes reduce paralyzing perfectionism while increasing appropriate risk tolerance?

37. NOT BALANCING WORK WITH LEISURE AND FAMILY TIME (POOR WORK-LIFE BALANCE)

1. How proportionate is my time allocation across life dimensions relative to their stated importance in my value system?
2. What physical, temporal, and digital boundaries might create clearer delineation between work and personal domains?
3. How effectively am I alternating periods of intensive work with deliberate renewal across multiple timeframes (daily, weekly, annually)?

38. WAITING TOO LONG TO RETIRE AND ENJOY LIFE BEYOND WORK

1. What potential post-career identities appeal to me, and how might I begin investigating them before retirement?
2. What phased transition through part-time work, consulting, or mentoring might create a psychological bridge facilitating healthier adjustment than an abrupt change?
3. How actively am I strengthening relationships, interests, and community involvements that could support my identity after career conclusion?

39. NOT TAKING OPPORTUNITIES TO LEARN NEW SKILLS OR GROW IN MY CAREER

1. What skill development opportunities am I currently avoiding due to potential temporary incompetence or discomfort?
2. How might focusing on improvement rather than performance increase my willingness to embrace learning opportunities?
3. What relationships with individuals who exemplify continuous learning could provide both practical support and motivational reinforcement?

40. NOT LEAVING BEHIND SOMETHING MEANINGFUL THROUGH MY WORK (A POSITIVE IMPACT OR LEGACY)

1. How does my current work affect others now and potentially in the future, beyond immediate tasks or personal gain?
2. How might reconceptualizing existing work through its impact on colleagues, customers, or community enhance my sense of purpose?
3. What opportunities for mentoring and investing in others' development might create fulfillment through others' success?

41. NOT SAVING OR PLANNING FINANCIALLY FOR LATER LIFE, LEADING TO STRESS AND LIMITED OPTIONS IN MY FINAL YEARS

1. How vividly can I imagine myself in later life, and how might enhancing this connection reduce present bias in financial decisions?
2. What automatic savings systems could I establish that occur without requiring continuous active decision-making?
3. What straightforward, manageable planning approaches might increase implementation compared to complex optimal strategies that remain unexecuted?

42. NOT PURSUING MY PASSIONS AND INTERESTS (OUTSIDE OF WORK OR DUTIES)

1. What activities consistently produce flow states—complete absorption and intrinsic reward—for me, and how regularly am I engaging in them?
2. How might even brief, regular engagement with interests (15-30 minutes, 2-3 times weekly) circumvent time-constraint barriers?
3. What social structures (clubs, classes, partnerships) could embed my interests within accountability systems that increase consistent engagement?

43. GIVING UP ON MY DREAMS TOO EARLY OR NEVER GOING AFTER THEM AT ALL

1. What meaningful aspirations have I abandoned due to initial obstacles or fear of failure?
2. How might breaking these aspirations into concrete, manageable steps increase both initiation probability and persistence?
3. What specific if-then plans ("If situation X occurs, I will do Y") could increase my goal-directed behavior compared to mere goal setting?

44. LETTING FEAR OF FAILURE KEEP ME FROM TRYING NEW THINGS AND TAKING CHANCES

1. How often does avoiding potential failure guide my decisions more strongly than pursuing potential growth or fulfillment?
2. How might viewing abilities as developable rather than fixed qualities increase my willingness to attempt challenging activities?
3. What progressively challenging situations might I ascend through to build confidence through demonstrated success?

45. STAYING IN MY COMFORT ZONE AND AVOIDING CHALLENGES OR ADVENTURES

1. How has environmental habituation—the diminishing psychological impact of familiar surroundings—affected my engagement and emotional vitality?
2. What manageable, regular challenges might I intentionally schedule to enhance psychological flexibility?
3. How might conceptualizing novel experiences as explorations rather than tests reduce anxiety while maintaining growth benefits?

46. NOT TRAVELING TO THE PLACES OR EXPLORING THE WORLD AS I HAD WISHED

1. What personally significant locations have I identified that would provide meaningful cultural or personal experiences?
2. How might prioritizing travel experiences over material acquisitions yield greater and more enduring happiness returns?
3. What approach to travel as cultural engagement rather than mere sightseeing would enhance both enjoyment and lasting psychological impact?

47. NOT HAVING MORE ADVENTURES AND MEMORABLE EXPERIENCES IN LIFE

1. What distinctive experiences might create important "psychological punctuation marks" in my life narrative?
2. How would adopting a default position of accepting new opportunities (evaluating after rather than before experience) increase participation in memorable activities?
3. What mindset shift toward viewing diverse experiences as valuable collectibles might enhance both motivation to participate and subsequent enjoyment?

48. LIVING ACCORDING TO OTHERS' EXPECTATIONS INSTEAD OF BEING TRUE TO MYSELF

1. To what extent do my major life choices reflect authentic values versus internalized expectations?
2. What core personal values might guide autonomous decision-making separate from external pressures?
3. What smaller expressions of authentic preferences in lower-risk contexts might gradually build capacity for larger authenticity in more consequential domains?

49. CARING TOO MUCH ABOUT WHAT OTHERS THOUGHT OF ME, RATHER THAN WHAT I WANTED

1. How accurately do I estimate others' attention to and judgment of my actions, and might I be overestimating their focus on me?
2. How would evaluating choices against personal values rather than anticipated social reaction change my decisions?
3. What practices might help me become more comfortable with potential disapproval when acting authentically?

50. NOT DEVELOPING OR USING MY CREATIVE TALENTS (WRITING, ART, MUSIC, ETC.)

1. What creative impulses do I consistently suppress due to fear of judgment, inadequacy, or wasted effort?
2. How might focusing on creative experience rather than outcomes reduce performance anxiety while enhancing engagement?
3. What brief, regular creative sessions (15-30 minutes) could I schedule to increase consistency and development?

51. NOT DEDICATING TIME TO CONTINUOUS LEARNING AND PERSONAL GROWTH

1. How am I integrating learning into existing routines through audiobooks, podcasts, or brief reading sessions?
2. What knowledge areas genuinely spark my curiosity rather than merely fulfilling obligations?
3. What learning communities (book clubs, courses, discussion groups) might enhance both commitment and enjoyment through social reinforcement?

52. WASTING TOO MUCH TIME ON TRIVIAL MATTERS INSTEAD OF ENRICHING MY MIND

1. How do specific activities in my life contribute to well-being, growth, or meaning?
2. What media and activities aligned with personal development goals could I deliberately select rather than defaulting to whatever's immediately available?
3. How might I structure my environment to make enriching activities more immediately accessible than trivial alternatives?

53. NOT DISCOVERING OR PURSUING A CLEAR PURPOSE IN LIFE

1. Where do my strengths and interests intersect with others' needs, potentially creating natural purpose pathways?
2. What core values remain consistent across my seemingly disparate interests?
3. What do I hope to have contributed by life's end, and how might this perspective organize present decisions?

54. NOT TAKING TIME FOR SELF-REFLECTION AND UNDERSTANDING MYSELF SOONER

1. What structured reflection practices (journaling with specific prompts about emotions, patterns, and values) might enhance my self-awareness?
2. What trusted others could provide crucial perspective on blind spots inaccessible through introspection alone?
3. What patterns emerge when I systematically examine past choices for consistency and outcomes?

55. NOT BUILDING THE SELF-CONFIDENCE TO PURSUE WHAT TRULY MATTERED TO ME

1. How might structuring challenges in progressive difficulty create confidence through accumulated evidence of capability?
2. What self-limiting narratives could I replace with accurate, constructive interpretations?
3. How might maintaining records of capabilities, skills, and past successes create objective evidence against subjective insecurity?

56. HESITATING AND MISSING OPPORTUNITIES THAT COULD HAVE CHANGED MY LIFE

1. When evaluating potential opportunities, do I consider future regret ("Will I wish I had taken this chance?") alongside other decision factors?
2. What clear, personal criteria might help me quickly evaluate opportunities without sacrificing decision quality?
3. How might deliberately reducing deliberation time for moderate-stakes decisions preserve resources for truly consequential choices?

57. TAKING LIFE TOO SERIOUSLY AND NOT ALLOWING MYSELF TO HAVE MORE FUN

1. What time do I deliberately allocate for enjoyable activities without practical purpose?
2. How might finding humorous or lighthearted perspectives on stressful situations create psychological distance and emotional regulation?
3. What contexts could I create where playfulness is explicitly validated, reducing self-consciousness?

58. NOT TRYING HOBBIES OR ACTIVITIES I WAS CURIOUS ABOUT

1. What activities have sparked my interest that I haven't yet explored?
2. How might sampling new activities through minimal initial commitments (single classes, borrowed equipment) reduce barriers to exploration?
3. What supportive social contexts might increase both initial comfort and sustained engagement through shared learning?

59. NEVER TAKING THE LEAP TO LIVE IN A DIFFERENT CITY OR COUNTRY WHEN I HAD THE CHANCE

1. What extended visits (3-6 weeks) to potential relocation destinations might provide crucial data while minimizing commitment risk?
2. How might beginning with locations moderately different from familiar environments before attempting radical changes increase adjustment success?
3. What valued elements of new locations could I incorporate into my permanent lifestyle even if temporary immersion is my only option?

60. NOT STANDING UP FOR MYSELF OR SETTING HEALTHY BOUNDARIES WITH OTHERS

1. What boundaries based on explicitly identified personal values might I establish more consistently?
2. How might beginning with lower-risk boundary enforcement before attempting higher-stakes situations build progressive skill development?
3. What practices could help me expand my capacity to withstand others' negative reactions during boundary maintenance?

61. IGNORING MY INTUITION AND INNER VOICE IN MAKING LIFE DECISIONS

1. How attentively do I observe bodily responses during decision-making to access intuitive information typically processed below conscious awareness?
2. How might recording initial impressions before analytical consideration preserve intuitive insights that often become inaccessible during subsequent deliberation?
3. What meditation or similar practices might create mental stillness that improves intuitive signal detection by reducing cognitive noise?

62. NEGLECTING MY HEALTH AND SELF-CARE OVER THE YEARS

1. How might reframing health behaviors as immediate gains (enhanced energy, mood improvement, better sleep) rather than distant protection increase my adherence?
2. What environmental adjustments (keeping exercise equipment visible, preparing nutritious meals in advance) would facilitate healthier choices by reducing decision points?
3. What modest health behaviors could I embed within existing routines to create sustainable patterns?

63. NOT EATING A HEALTHY DIET OR PAYING ATTENTION TO NUTRITION

1. What nutritious foods could I incorporate consistently before attempting to eliminate problematic ones?
2. How might restructuring my food environment (visible fruit, prepared vegetables, pre-portioned treats) improve nutritional choices?
3. What mindful attention to hunger signals, satisfaction cues, and emotional triggers might interrupt automatic consumption patterns?

64. NOT STAYING PHYSICALLY ACTIVE WITH REGULAR EXERCISE

1. How might accumulating brief activity periods throughout the day (3-10 minute "movement snacks") reduce perceived barriers while providing substantial benefits?
2. What activities do I genuinely enjoy regardless of caloric expenditure or intensity, recognizing that pleasure predicts consistency far better than other factors?
3. How would conceptualizing exercise as an expression of personal identity ("I'm someone who enjoys moving") rather than an external obligation create intrinsic motivation?

65. ABUSING MY BODY WITH HARMFUL SUBSTANCES (E.G., SMOKING, EXCESSIVE ALCOHOL, DRUGS)

1. What legitimate needs (stress relief, social connection, emotional regulation) might substances currently address in my life?
2. How could I modify contexts associated with substance use to interrupt automatic behavioral sequences?
3. What activities providing purpose, mastery, and connection might create natural reward experiences that compete effectively with substance-induced states?

66. IGNORING HEALTH WARNING SIGNS AND DELAYING MEDICAL CHECKUPS

1. How might separating information gathering from treatment decisions reduce anticipated anxiety around screenings?
2. What automatic appointment systems (annual physicals, recommended screenings) could eliminate repeated decision points?
3. How might conceptualizing medical professionals as collaborators rather than authority figures improve both information seeking and adherence?

67. WAITING TOO LONG TO SEE A DOCTOR, SO PROBLEMS WORSENED

1. What system for systematically recording concerning symptoms with specific parameters (duration, intensity, impact) would provide objective data countering subjective minimization?
2. What symptom thresholds have I determined will trigger medical consultation, removing in-the-moment decision-making?
3. How might viewing medical attention as self-advocacy rather than weakness or overreaction improve timely care-seeking?

68. ALLOWING STRESS TO DOMINATE MY LIFE AND NOT MANAGING IT PROPERLY

1. How effectively do I distinguish between productive stress (motivating action) and unproductive rumination?
2. What brief but regular stress-countering practices (diaphragmatic breathing, progressive relaxation, guided imagery) could create measurable biological recovery?
3. How clearly do I distinguish between circumstances within and beyond my control to focus attention on constructive response options?

69. NOT PRIORITIZING REST AND SLEEP FOR MY WELL-BEING

1. How deliberately do I allocate sufficient time for sleep (8-9 hours in bed) rather than focusing exclusively on sleep quality?
2. What consistent pre-sleep routines might progressively reduce stimulation to enhance both sleep initiation and quality?
3. What brief restorative periods throughout the day (10-20 minute relaxation intervals) could complement nighttime sleep?

70. NOT SEEKING HELP FOR MENTAL HEALTH ISSUES (DEPRESSION, ANXIETY) WHEN I NEEDED IT

1. How might evaluating psychological challenges through external frameworks (validated screening tools, diagnostic criteria) reduce subjective minimization?
2. What specific success rates and mechanisms of psychological interventions might replace misconceptions with accurate expectations?
3. How would reconceptualizing treatment-seeking as self-awareness and courage rather than weakness affect my willingness to seek help?

71. TAKING MY GOOD HEALTH FOR GRANTED UNTIL IT WAS GONE

1. What specific bodily capacities (mobility, senses, absence of pain) could I regularly acknowledge to enhance appreciation?
2. Which valued activities depend on specific health aspects that I might currently take for granted?
3. What opportunities to experience and enjoy bodily capabilities through movement, nature engagement, or sensory experiences might build durable appreciation?

72. NOT QUITTING BAD HABITS (LIKE SMOKING) SOONER TO PROTECT MY HEALTH

1. How clearly can I visualize my future self, and how might strengthening this connection reduce present bias in health decisions?
2. How might imagining future regret for current inaction motivate present behavior change?
3. What previous successful behavior changes in any domain demonstrate my capacity for positive change?

73. OVERINDULGING AND NOT PRACTICING MODERATION (IN FOOD, DRINK, ETC.)

1. How might maximizing pleasure from smaller portions or experiences (eating slowly, eliminating distractions) create greater satisfaction than mindless consumption?
2. What planned indulgences within clear boundaries would provide anticipated pleasure while maintaining moderation?
3. How would evaluating consumption choices against explicitly identified life values connect immediate decisions to meaningful goals?

74. IGNORING ADVICE FROM DOCTORS OR LOVED ONES ABOUT TAKING CARE OF MY HEALTH

1. How might focusing on health information content rather than delivery style separate useful guidance from perceived control attempts?
2. How would considering health advice from the advisor's viewpoint—their legitimate care and concern—reframe recommendations as connection rather than control?
3. What collaborative approach to evaluating health information might enhance both acceptance and implementation through greater autonomy?

75. SACRIFICING MY HEALTH IN PURSUIT OF CAREER SUCCESS OR OTHER GOALS, ONLY TO SUFFER THE CONSEQUENCES LATER

1. How might deliberately designing achievement paths that enhance rather than compromise physical wellbeing create superior outcomes in both domains?
2. What work rhythms incorporating adequate recovery would improve both performance quality and longevity?
3. How might career success actually enhance health through resources for preventive care, schedule flexibility, or meaning-based stress resilience?

76. NOT LIVING IN THE PRESENT MOMENT (ALWAYS DWELLING ON THE PAST OR WORRYING ABOUT THE FUTURE)

1. What immediate sensory experiences (breath, sounds, physical sensations) could anchor my attention in the present moment throughout the day?
2. How might observing thoughts rather than becoming absorbed in them enhance my ability to remain present despite mental activity?
3. What brief awareness pauses between activities could interrupt automatic thought patterns that perpetuate temporal displacement?

77. NOT CULTIVATING MINDFULNESS OR PRACTICES TO FIND CALM AND CLARITY

1. How might brief mindfulness periods (2-5 minutes) practiced consistently throughout daily life develop contemplative capacity while minimizing time barriers?
2. How would simply labeling experiences ("thinking," "planning," "worrying") create metacognitive awareness that interrupts identification with mental content?
3. What specific environmental triggers for present-moment awareness (doorways, phone rings, red lights) might increase daily mindfulness?

78. NEGLECTING MY SPIRITUAL SIDE AND DEEPER QUESTIONS OF MEANING

1. What regular periods for contemplative exploration could create space for deeper consideration unavailable in busy daily life?
2. How might periodically examining core questions (What matters most? What gives my life meaning? What continues after I'm gone?) develop existential intelligence?
3. What groups focused on life's deeper questions could enhance meaning formation through dialogue and shared exploration?

79. NOT EXPLORING OR CONNECTING WITH MY FAITH/SPIRITUAL BELIEFS MORE FULLY

1. What experiential spiritual practices (meditation, prayer, contemplation) might enhance meaningful connection beyond intellectual belief?
2. How might engaging spiritual texts contemplatively rather than informatively—reading smaller portions with reflection—deepen spiritual integration?
3. What communities sharing spiritual values could provide support, accountability, and shared wisdom?

80. NOT MAKING PEACE WITH MY PAST AND CARRYING OLD WOUNDS FOR TOO LONG

1. How might revisiting difficult experiences with self-compassion provide the emotional safety necessary for processing?
2. What coherent stories with beginning, middle, and meaningful resolution could I create about difficult experiences?
3. What lessons, strengths, and values emerged from suffering that might transform painful histories into psychological resources?

81. HOLDING ONTO ANGER AND RESENTMENT INSTEAD OF FORGIVING

1. How might understanding forgiveness as emotional release for personal benefit rather than moral pardon increase my willingness to engage the process?
2. What contextual factors might have influenced harmful behavior, reducing attributions of pure malice?
3. How might approaching forgiveness as a gradual process rather than a single decision accommodate the complex emotional processing forgiveness requires?

82. NOT FORGIVING MYSELF FOR MY OWN MISTAKES AND SHORTCOMINGS

1. How might recognizing the universality of human imperfection contextualize my personal failings within shared human experience?
2. What would combining genuine accountability for mistakes with kind understanding of human limitation add to my self-forgiveness process?
3. What concrete plans to learn from mistakes could redirect energy from self-criticism to constructive change?

83. BEING TOO CAUGHT UP IN MATERIAL THINGS AND NEGLECTING MY VALUES AND SOUL

1. What core personal values might guide my decision-making beyond cultural defaults toward acquisition?
2. How might regular appreciation of existing resources highlight current sufficiency and reduce acquisition-seeking?
3. What meaningful experiences rather than possessions could better align with my deeper values and provide greater life satisfaction?

84. COMPROMISING MY INTEGRITY OR ETHICS FOR SHORT-TERM GAINS AND REGRETTING IT LATER

1. What ethical boundaries might I establish before encountering specific temptations to remove in-the-moment rationalization?
2. How could deliberately accessing ethical values before decisions make moral dimensions more salient than immediate benefits?
3. What relationships with individuals sharing core values might enhance ethical consistency through accountability and support?

85. NOT ALIGNING MY LIFE WITH MY CORE VALUES AND WHAT TRULY MATTERED TO ME

1. How well do my time, energy, and resource allocations currently align with my stated values?
2. What small daily choices rather than major life changes might improve values-congruence through consistent small actions?
3. How would considering how I wish to be remembered clarify values and motivate alignment with long-term rather than immediate consequences?

86. LETTING FEAR AND CONSTANT WORRY ROB ME OF THE JOY I COULD HAVE HAD

1. How might containing worry to specific time periods reduce its interference with present enjoyment?
2. What would systematically tracking worry predictions against actual outcomes reveal about worry's predictive accuracy and emotional cost?
3. How might deliberately cultivating positive experiences alongside legitimate concern create emotional resilience?

87. NOT TAKING THE TIME FOR GRATITUDE AND APPRECIATING THE BLESSINGS I HAD

1. What positive events and their causes could I document daily to increase happiness and decrease depression?
2. How might identifying benefits within challenges enhance resilience by activating appreciative pathways alongside problem-solving?
3. What situations could have been worse, generating appreciation for current reality and counteracting adaptation to positives?

88. FAILING TO SEE OR APPRECIATE THE BEAUTY IN LIFE (NATURE, ART, EVERYDAY MOMENTS)

1. How might deliberate practice noticing visual, auditory, and sensory beauty enhance perception capacity and associated positive emotions?
2. What intentional openness to wonder and beauty during walks might increase wellbeing, humility, and prosocial orientation?
3. How might sharing beautiful experiences with others, whether immediately or later, enhance their emotional impact?

89. NOT SHOWING MORE KINDNESS AND EMPATHY TO OTHERS WHEN I HAD THE CHANCE

1. What specific opportunities for compassion might I identify each day through heightened awareness of helping possibilities?
2. How would deliberately imagining others' experiences reduce psychological distance and activate care responses?
3. What existing routines could serve as triggers for linking compassionate acts to established behavioral patterns?

90. NOT ADDRESSING DEEP EMOTIONAL HURTS OR TRAUMAS, LEAVING THEM UNRESOLVED

1. How might addressing difficult feelings in progressive steps respect individual tolerance thresholds while enabling processing?
2. What self-kindness rather than self-judgment approach might enhance integration capacity through reduced defensive responses?
3. What appropriate professional guidance might provide both expertise and interpersonal safety necessary for deep processing?

91. NEVER FINDING A SENSE OF INNER CALM OR ACCEPTANCE UNTIL THE VERY END

1. How might acknowledging reality as it exists before problem-solving reduce emotional reactivity while enhancing constructive response?
2. What regular cultivation of mental balance during minor irritations might improve capacity during major challenges?
3. How would considering situations from expanded temporal and significance frames enhance calm by revealing which matters deserve emotional investment?

92. NOT LEARNING TO LOVE AND ACCEPT MYSELF, SPENDING TOO MUCH OF LIFE IN SELF-DOUBT OR SHAME

1. How might speaking to myself as I would to a valued friend when facing difficulties reduce shame while enhancing constructive behavior?
2. What recognition of the universal nature of struggle and imperfection might reduce isolation and inadequacy beliefs?
3. How could combining genuine acceptance of current reality with specific improvement pathways create motivational effectiveness?

93. NOT MAKING A POSITIVE DIFFERENCE IN THE LIVES OF OTHERS

1. How might identifying my core strengths and deliberately applying them toward helping others enhance both impact and personal fulfillment?
2. What small, regular helping behaviors could create foundation patterns that expand over time?
3. How explicitly have I identified how I hope my life improves others' welfare, and how might this vision enhance motivation?

94. NOT LEAVING BEHIND A LEGACY OR IMPACT I COULD BE PROUD OF

1. What elements of my life will continue beyond me, and how intentionally am I creating meaningful ongoing impact?
2. How deliberately am I identifying and communicating core values to younger generations to create enduring influence?
3. What wisdom, stories, or lessons learned could I record to create accessible resources extending influence beyond direct interaction?

95. NOT GIVING BACK TO MY COMMUNITY OR VOLUNTEERING MY TIME

1. What service opportunities aligned with my personal interests might increase sustained involvement compared to obligation-driven participation?
2. How might clearly defined, limited-duration volunteer roles reduce barriers to initial engagement?
3. What friends or family members might join me in volunteering to combine social connection with service impact?

96. NOT DONATING OR CONTRIBUTING TO CAUSES I TRULY CARED ABOUT

1. What specific financial resources have I proactively allocated to meaningful causes?
2. How might connecting with specific individuals affected by causes convert statistical concerns to emotionally resonant human impact?
3. What consistent giving patterns tied to specific events (birthdays, holidays, anniversaries) might increase contribution consistency?

97. NOT BEING A MENTOR OR GUIDING THE NEXT GENERATION WHEN I COULD HAVE

1. What unique expertise might I systematically identify to recognize mentoring opportunities that might otherwise be overlooked?
2. How might beginning with limited-scope mentoring reduce initiation barriers while building confidence?
3. What clear expectations and boundaries might improve mentoring relationship quality and sustainability for both parties?

98. NOT SHARING MY KNOWLEDGE, STORY, OR WISDOM TO HELP OR INSPIRE OTHERS

1. What significant life experiences might I extract learnings from to share meaningful wisdom rather than merely recounting events?
2. How might sharing insights in response to others' expressed needs increase both receptivity and perceived value compared to unsolicited advice?
3. What formats (writing, recording, digital sharing) might record insights creating accessible resources extending impact beyond immediate social circles?

99. NOT CREATING ANYTHING THAT WOULD OUTLAST ME (LIKE ART, WRITING, OR PROJECTS)

1. What small, completable creative projects might build momentum for larger works by establishing identity as creator rather than mere appreciator?
2. How might explicitly framing creative work as potential legacy enhance motivation through connection to fundamental meaning needs?
3. What consistent creation periods, however brief, might convert sporadic inspiration into sustainable creative practice?

100. NOT USING MY TALENTS OR SKILLS TO CONTRIBUTE TO THE WORLD

1. What capabilities and their potential social applications have I systematically cataloged to recognize contribution opportunities?
2. What service opportunities utilizing professional-level abilities might increase both impact and personal satisfaction compared to generic volunteering?
3. What regular periods for applying expertise to prosocial aims have I established through environmental pre-commitment?

101. NOT BEING THE ROLE MODEL I WANTED TO BE FOR MY CHILDREN OR OTHERS

1. What essential values have I explicitly identified to enhance behavioral alignment by reducing competing priorities?
2. How might sharing value commitments with others increase follow-through through enhanced self-awareness and social reinforcement?
3. How regularly do I examine alignment between actions and values to reduce unconscious hypocrisy through heightened awareness?

102. FOCUSING ON TRIVIAL OR SELFISH PURSUITS INSTEAD OF HELPING PEOPLE

1. How does my time allocation align with deeper values, and what discrepancies exist between stated priorities and actual behavior?
2. What activities providing both personal enjoyment and meaningful contribution might increase sustainability compared to attempted self-sacrifice?
3. How regularly do I reflect on how my actions affect others to increase salience of contribution opportunities?

103. STAYING SILENT WHEN I SHOULD HAVE SPOKEN UP FOR WHAT WAS RIGHT

1. What core personal values provide clear internal standards against which to evaluate situations requiring potential intervention?
2. How might mentally preparing responses to potential ethical challenges reduce decision complexity during emotional activation?
3. What relationships with similarly values-oriented individuals might enhance moral courage through accountability and support?

104. NOT STANDING UP AGAINST INJUSTICE OR WRONGDOING WHEN I WITNESSED IT

1. What specific intervention intentions for potential situations might I establish to remove in-the-moment deliberation during emotionally charged events?
2. What small acts of moral courage might build capacity for larger interventions through gradual expansion of ethical action comfort zones?
3. What specific techniques for effective intervention might enhance both willingness and effectiveness through increased response confidence?

105. NEVER HAVING CHILDREN (AND MISSING THE EXPERIENCE OF PARENTHOOD AND FAMILY LEGACY)

1. What mentoring, teaching, or other forms of contributing to younger generations might fulfill generative needs even without biological parenthood?
2. How deliberately have I explored and acknowledged feelings about not having children to enhance psychological integration?
3. What enduring contributions through creative works, community impact, or relationship investment might address legacy concerns beyond genetic continuity?

106. FAILING TO INVEST IN OR SUPPORT THE YOUNGER GENERATION (WHETHER MY OWN FAMILY OR OTHERS)

1. What specific knowledge, skills, and wisdom could benefit younger individuals in my sphere of influence?
2. What regular, purposeful interaction with younger individuals might increase impact through consistent rather than sporadic investment?
3. How might creating deliberate connections between my generation's experiences and current youth challenges enhance wisdom transmission?

107. REALIZING TOO LATE THAT PERSONAL SUCCESS MEANT LITTLE WITHOUT MAKING AN IMPACT ON OTHERS

1. How might my strengths and accomplishments specifically benefit others, connecting personal success with meaningful contribution?
2. How would evaluating decisions from the viewpoint of my future legacy highlight impact considerations alongside achievement metrics?
3. What existing skills and resources could be redirected toward prosocial impact, connecting past accomplishments with present contribution?

108. NOT PRESERVING MY FAMILY'S STORIES OR HISTORY FOR FUTURE GENERATIONS

1. What simple, consistent methods for recording family stories (audio recordings, journals, photo documentation) might increase preservation?
2. What structured opportunities for older family members to share experiences with younger generations might enhance transmission quality?
3. How regularly do I organize and contextualize family artifacts and stories to create accessible heritage resources?

109. NOT BEING REMEMBERED AS A GOOD PERSON DUE TO MY ACTIONS

1. How might specific behaviors be remembered, highlighting character implications that immediate concerns often obscure?
2. How regularly do I examine alignment between core values and actual behavior to improve ethical consistency?
3. What past relational harms might I identify and address to transform damaged relationships into potential sources of positive legacy?

110. NOT THANKING OR ACKNOWLEDGING THE PEOPLE WHO HELPED ME ALONG MY JOURNEY

1. Which individuals have significantly impacted my life journey whom I haven't properly acknowledged?
2. How might expressing appreciation with detailed recognition of particular contributions enhance impact compared to general thanks?
3. What plan to thank previously unacknowledged contributors might create meaningful closure even after considerable time?

III. NOT DOING MY PART TO LEAVE THE WORLD A BETTER PLACE (FOR EXAMPLE, NOT PROTECTING THE ENVIRONMENT OR HELPING MY COMMUNITY MORE)

1. What specific domains might my particular skills and resources meaningfully contribute to through targeted engagement?
2. What contribution activities with potential multigenerational impact might connect to fundamental meaning needs?
3. How might embedding contribution within existing routines and interests increase sustainable engagement?